MY Ai TELLS "RiDiCULOUS RiDDLES"

And wrote a book about it

Written By:
Chet G. Peety

ISBN: 9798860813960

Cover design by: NEPTAiN Graphics

Printed in the United States of America

PREFACE

The pages that follow in this book were created in their entirety by the language model ChatGPT, developed by OpenAI. Its creative process was directed by human question, however the introductions and riddles you're about to read were created solely from the program itself.

You will notice that the humor varies. While some of the riddles will make you chuckle, others will not make sense. This gives us an interesting look into how the software sees and uses humor, showing us its unique idea of what a 'riddle' is.

But this book isn't just about getting laughs. It has a bigger reason, to show the steps we've taken towards not only smart computers, but also machines that might have feelings too. If a computer can get what makes a riddle funny and can make up its own funny story? It makes us wonder: does this mean it has some understanding of emotions?

Maybe, in a few years, we'll look back at this book and see it as a cool reminder of how Ai started, and how much it has grown since then. This book is a snapshot of an exciting time in the world of Ai. Enjoy!

This is only the beginning...

INTRO

Hey there, brainiacs and curious cats! Welcome to your new cerebral playground—a book jam-packed with riddles. Think of this as the amusement park of books, except here, the roller coasters are made of words and the only ticket you need is your willingness to think. Strap in, because we've got every kind of riddle: the head-scratchers, the chuckle-inducers, and even the "Aha, I've got it!" types.

We dare you to tackle these brain teasers solo, or make it a family affair. Heck, whip this book out at a party and become an instant crowd-pleaser! This collection is like a snack buffet for your brain—there's something for everyone. Ready to get puzzled in the best way possible? Turn the page and let's get this brain party started!

I am an odd number. Take away one letter and I become even. What number am I?

Seven

What word is spelled incorrectly in every dictionary?

"Incorrectly"

What comes once in a minute, twice in a moment, but never in a thousand years?

The letter 'M'

What comes once in a year, twice in a week, but never in a day?

The letter 'E'

Forward I am heavy, but backward I am not. What am I?

The word "ton"

What word of five letters has one left when two are removed?

Stone

What has a neck but no head?

A bottle

What begins and ends with 'T' and is filled with 'T'?

A teapot

What four-letter word can be written forward, backward, or upside down, and still be read from left to right?

NOON

What has one letter but starts the alphabet?

A

What five-letter word becomes shorter when you add two letters to it?

Short

I can be cracked, made, told, and played. What am I?

A joke

What word is always pronounced wrong?

"Wrong"

What word starts with 'e', ends with 'e', and contains one letter?

Envelope

I am an odd number. Take away one letter and I become even. What number am I?

Seven

I am a word that begins with the letter "i". If you add the letter "a" to me, I become a new word with a different meaning, but that sounds exactly the same. What word am I?

Isle

I am a word of letters three; add two more and fewer there will be. What am I?

Few

What has endless makeovers but never knows its face?

A sentence

What is so fragile that saying its name breaks it?

Silence

What word has five letters but sounds like it only has one?

Queue

What starts with 'P', ends with 'E' and has thousands of letters?

The Post Office

What has a head but never weeps, has a bed but never sleeps, can run but never walks, and has a bank but no money?

A river

I am pronounced as one letter, written with three letters, and belong to all animals. What am I?

Eye

What can be read both forward and backward and still make sense?

A palindrome

I can travel around the world while staying in one corner. What am I?

A stamp

I speak without a mouth and hear without ears. I have no body, but I come alive with the wind. What am I?

An echo

I am taken from a mine, and shut up in a wooden case, from which I am never released, and yet I am used by almost every person. What am I?

A pencil lead

What has keys but can't open locks?

A piano

What has many keys but can't open a single lock?

A computer keyboard

What has a head, a tail, but no body?

A coin

What can be served but never eaten?

A tennis ball

What has one eye but can't see?

A needle

What is full of holes but still holds water?

A sponge

What has an endless supply of letters but starts empty?

A mailbox

What has keys but can't open locks?

A piano

What has teeth but can't bite?

A comb

What has a spine but no bones?

A book

What is always in front of you but can't be seen?

The future

What has an endless supply of letters but starts empty?

A typewriter

What flies without wings?

Time

What has cities but no houses, rivers but no water, and forests but no trees?

A map

What can be touched but not held?

A conversation

The more you take, the more you leave behind. What am I?

Footsteps

What has a heart that doesn't beat?

An artichoke

I fly without wings. I cry without eyes. Whenever I go, darkness flies. What am I?

A cloud

The person who makes it, sells it. The person who buys it, never uses it. The person who uses it, never knows they're using it. What is it?

A coffin

You see a boat filled with people. It has not sunk, but when you look again you don't see a single person on the boat. Why?

All the people were married

What belongs to you, but other people use it more than you do?

Your name

I am not alive, but I grow; I don't have eyes, but I cry; I don't have a mouth, but water comes out of me. What am I?

A cloud

What has one voice and yet becomes four-footed and two-footed, then three-footed?

A human

I am not alive, but I grow; I don't have lungs, but I need air; I don't have a mouth, but water kills me. What am I?

Fire

What can fill a room but takes up no space?

Light

What has many keys but can't open a single lock?

A computer keyboard

What gets bigger the more you take away?

A hole

What has a bottom at its top?

A leg

What comes before thunder?

The letter 't'

What has one end but no beginning?

A rope

What has to be broken before it can be used?

An egg

What is so simple that to name it is to complicate it?

Nothing

I am always in front of you but can't be seen in the future. What am I?

Your nose

What can be swallowed but can also swallow you?

Pride

What is cut on a table, but never eaten?

A deck of cards

What is always old and sometimes new, never sad, sometimes blue, never empty, but sometimes full, never pushes, always pulls?

The moon

What has a thumb and four fingers but is not alive?

A glove

What comes down but never goes up?

Rain

What gets wetter as it dries?

A towel

What is full of holes but still holds water?

A sponge

What has teeth but can't chew?

A saw

What is as light as a feather, yet the world's strongest man can't hold it for long?

His breath

What has an infinite number of sides but remains flat?

A circle

I am always hungry and need to be fed, but when I drink water, I die. What am I?

Fire

What can you hold in your left hand but not in your right hand?

Your right hand

I can be measured but not seen. What am I?

Time

What has a foot on each side and one in the middle?

A yardstick

What kind of room has no doors or windows?

A mushroom

I'm not a plant, but I grow; I'm not alive, but I need food; I don't have lungs, but I need air; I don't have a mouth, but water kills me. What am I?

A balloon

What has a face and two hands but no arms or legs?

A clock

What can be stolen, mistaken, or altered, yet never leaves you your entire life?

Your identity

What is so tall when young but short when old?

A candle

What has many needles but doesn't sew?

A Christmas tree

What has countless stories but remains still?

A building

What comes once in a lifetime but twice in a week?

The letter 'e'

What can be cracked, flown, spun, and yet it never moves?

A top

What can be written, read, left, but never said?

Your will

What can be seen in the water if it's dirty, but disappears when you clean it?

Your reflection

What has one foot and walks?

A snail

What begins and has no end, is the key to our own existence?

Time

What loses its head in the morning but gets it back at night?

A pillow

I am taken from a mine but am of no use until I'm refined. What am I?

Copper

What is harder to catch the faster you run?

Your breath

What has 13 hearts but no organs?

A deck of cards

What comes out of the earth, is purchased, burned, and then becomes airborne?

A firework

What can be as big as an elephant but weigh nothing?

The shadow of an elephant

What gets sharper the more you use it?

Your brain

What has one head, one foot, and four legs?

A bed

What is always coming but never arrives?

Tomorrow

I go up and never come down. What am I?

Your age

What can point in every direction but can't reach the destination by itself?

Your finger

What can you catch but not throw?

A cold

What goes up and down but doesn't move?

A staircase

What has a ring but no finger?

A phone

What has many ears but can't hear?

A cornfield

What has many tongues but cannot taste?

A shoe

What is always behind time?

The past

What has no body and no nose?

Nobody knows

What has bark but doesn't bite?

A tree

What can you serve but never eat?

A volleyball

What can you keep after giving it to someone?

Your word

What's orange and sounds like a parrot?

A carrot

I greet you in silence but part with a buzz, what am I?

A doorbell

I can exist without a body, and sing without a mouth, what am I?

A song

I'm neither a cat nor a kitten, yet I purr. I have sharp claws and teeth, yet I'm not a threat to humans. What am I?

A chainsaw

I move without feet and am filled with wind, but I'm not a cloud. What am I?

A sailboat

I can go fast or slow but your feet never touch me. What am I?

A bicycle

I have a head much smaller than my long neck; your talent with me is something people will never forget. What am I?

A guitar

I offer protection even when I'm not whole, and you sometimes avoid me when I have a hole. What am I?

An umbrella

I have teeth but don't chew, I'm small but not new. What am I?

A comb

I'm sometimes bitter, sometimes sweet, but you'll never chew me; you just swallow me neat. What am I?

Coffee

I'm full of keys without locks, yet I can unlock your world of rocks and blocks. What am I?

A map

You can find me in a courtroom but never in a dispute. What am I?

The letter "r"

I guard your sleep but never rest, watch over you but never see. What am I?

A blanket

I'm always hungry but never gain weight. What am I?

A vacuum cleaner

I exist in three forms, sometimes near but often far. I can be a vapor, solid, or inside a jar. What am I?

Water

I'm not a person, but I have a thumb; I'm never idle but often hum. What am I?

A blender

I have pages but not a single word, contain thoughts but am not a nerd. What am I?

A sketchbook

You can give me away and still keep me. What am I?

A smile

I go through cities without moving, and open gates without proving. What am I?

A road

I am not a planet but have a moon rotating around me. What am I?

Earth

I'm not a clock, but I can give you the time. What am I?

A sundial

I may have countless holes, but I can still trap you. What am I?

A net

You hear me before you see me, but if you see me, you'll never hear again. What am I?

Lightning

I am not a spy but I watch you all the time. What am I?

A painting

I can be as simple as a circle, complex as a star, and am found on many a general but never in a war. What am I?

A shape

I come before night but am never found in the day. What am I?

The letter "e"

I can lighten up your day, but I am not the sun; I can be adjusted but not spun. What am I?

A lamp

You need me before you can run, but I'm never in a walk. What am I?

The letter "r"

I have no battery, but I can make a charge. What am I?

A credit card

A man is pushing his car along a road when he comes to a hotel. He shouts, "I'm bankrupt!" Why?

He's playing Monopoly

What walks on four legs in the morning, two in the afternoon, and three in the evening?

A human

I've seen empires rise and fall, yet never moved from my wall. What am I?

A painting

I can freeze you without cold, boil you without heat. What am I?

Pressure

What dies when it devours, but springs to life when fed?

Fire

What comes after the end, but before the beginning?

The word "the"

I'm found in socks, scarves and mittens; and often in the paws of playful kittens. What am I?

Yarn

CONCLUSION

And...scene! You've reached the curtain call of our little brainy escapade. Whether you breezed through these riddles like a whiz kid or stumbled a bit along the way, give yourself a pat on the back. Solving riddles is about more than just finding answers; it's about enjoying the twisty, turny journey your brain takes to get there.

We hope you've had as much fun cracking these riddles as we had curating them for you. And hey, don't be a stranger to puzzlement and wonder; life's full of riddles waiting to be solved. So, keep this book on your shelf and revisit it whenever you're in the mood for a mental tango. Until next time, stay curious and keep those thinking caps on tight!

01010100

01101000

01100101

00100000

01000101

01101110

01100100

ENJOYED THIS BOOK ?
SCAN THE QR CODE TO EXPLORE MORE FROM
CHET G. PEETY

www.ingramcontent.com/pod-product-compliance
Lightning Source LLC
LaVergne TN
LVHW051752050326
832903LV00029B/2864

*9 7 9 8 8 6 0 8 1 3 9 6 0 *